N

PROMISES

A POETRY COLLECTION

Danah Slade

ISBN 978-1-76350-050-1

Cover Art by Glam Beckett

Internal Illustrations by Danah Slade

Obsidian Moth Publishing

For all enquiries email: slade.enquiries@gmail.com

Table of Contents

Falling

Fractured

Facing

Preface

Dear Reader,

Before I begin this collection, it's important I give you some context. I began writing this poetry collection at 14 years-old and have been building on it ever since. While this may not be the most sophisticated of my works, I wanted to share a story of growth with you.

Around the age of seven, I was diagnosed with dyslexia, I couldn't read, spell or do maths. Now, at age 22, I still can't do maths.... but my poetry has appeared in publications such as 'Australian Poetry Journal', 'Beyond Queer Words' and 'StylusLit'. I frequent open mics and have performed in the Adelaide and Edinburgh Fringe Festivals.

As a member of the queer community, I'm aware poetry offers a sanctuary for voices that are often marginalised. I've seen the way poetry can amplify these voices, uplift, challenge stereotypes and confront injustices. In my own life, it's been a vessel for me to abolish limitations placed upon me. Whether it's social constructs, relating to my gender and sexuality, or learning and health disabilities.

After being diagnosed with dyslexia, I was offered many resources, none of which truly helped. This was up until the point my mother put me through the Davis Dyslexia Program. The program taught me literacy through visualisation and kinesiology. Today, my learning disability isn't as noticeable but it hasn't disappeared either. It means I take longer to process information than most people, but I'm also more aware of how to navigate dyslexia's advantages.

Since I've grown up processing words through my senses, this has reflected in my writing style. Within this collection, you may notice the correlations between words I've selected. Most people are aware dyslexia affects how an individual distinguishes similarly spelt words. However, I wanted to show the way our brains overlay the meanings and imagery of words too. As a writer, to embrace the natural patterns of a neuro-diverse brain is to exhibit how poetry is never a 2D experience.

Through the practice of writing, I've gained great clarity in my personal life. I admit at the beginning, I was conflicted about calling myself a part of the poetry community. Not only as a dyslexic but because there's a sappy stereotype associated with the word 'poet'. This introspection led me on the pursuit of redefining the most prevalent poetry genres, 'love' and ‘heartbreak’. The cynical romanticist style I’ve chosen to adopt in ‘No Promises’ is a direct response to this.

While this collection isn’t in chronological order, you can see the ways my skills developed over eight years. I attempt to balance accessible language with unique imagery. I note the role ‘relatability’ plays in modern poetry, the space for personal interpretation, whilst also considering how much more immersive and impactful personal stories can be within our communities.

There are four sections in ‘No Promises’ signifying the stages of a break-up. These include ‘Falling’, ‘Fractured’, ‘Fighting’ and ‘Facing’. ‘Falling’ speaks of the naivety of love and subsequently, the way relationships can quickly turn bitter. ‘Fractured’ is the open wound of this collection, where we find ourselves stuck in our emotional body. ‘Fighting’ is about breaking free from our attachments usually by transforming pain into anger. ‘Facing’ is when I reflect on the roles we played in our own suffering, to then take responsibility of our healing.

I advise readers to explore this collection in whatever manner suits them, whether it’s closing their eyes and flipping to a random page, selecting a section they feel most called-to or reading it cover-to-cover. I hope ‘No Promises’ contributes to readers wellbeing in some way – may it be a comfort or a wake-up call.

Yours,
Danah

Dedicated to beginner poetry readers,
specifically, my younger sister.

Trigger Warning:
mentions of domestic violence and suicide.

Falling

MORE EDGES THAN BEFORE

2021

I folded my heart up years ago.
Its creases have worn,
disintegrated
and as I open it before you
it falls apart,
more edges than before.

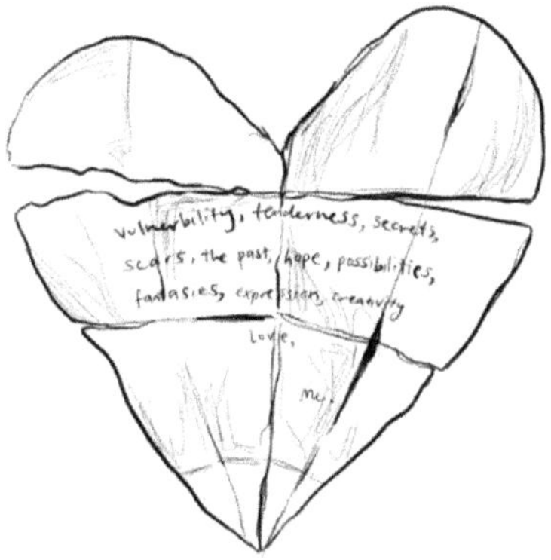
vulnerbility, tenderness, secrets,
scars, the past, hope, possibilities,
fantasies, expression, creativity
love,
me.

TRATAK KRIYA

2023

In practising the meditation technique, Tratak Kriya
I learnt, if you stare at something too long
it disappears,
as if an illusion all along.

I am since apprehensive;
if I put too much attention into us
reality will surely swallow you.

Though, I can't blink when
we are all destined for yesterday.

What is more foolish –

believing physics backflips and breaks
it's neck before me?
As if it were simpler to be chosen by the universe
than any one person on earth –

Or the fact, I would keenly give up
any supernaturality
to age mundanely with you?

DEPENDABLE END

2024

My Rock,
My Morning Star,
My Iron Will,
My Blunt-force Charity,
My Point-blank Beauty.

If you must be
my most dependable end,
let me call you by it.

May you know – as I stand before you –
I'm fully aware
of the mobility in my two legs,
of the exits,
of how soluble time could be.

But I look at you.
The rims of my iris – circles
in the lake
of your anticipated impact.

I look at you
the same way a target board asks,
'give me a point'.

NEVER FALL IN LOVE WITH ME
2023

Never fall in love with me.

I will kiss you like a draft

in hopes there's no finality.

I will rewrite and rewrite and rewrite us

until we are all an asphyxiated world
knows of the trees.

I said, I will kiss you like a *draught*

emerging from nowhere...

when you're doing the dishes,

making coffee

and brushing your teeth.

Which is to say,
I will hold you up –

I will hold you up
like a stone to the light.

And after the inevitable,
once your ebullient refractions

turn

to

retractions.

When you're spitting in a porcelain sink,

clipping your nails

or washing *your* sheets.

In those – most ordinary moments –
you'll marry anticipation...

leave doors open just a crack,

noticing how cold it is,
once I've mirrored your avoidance.

A FAILED FRENCH EXIT

M.B. / September 2023

(The city of) love is crowded
fashionable,
polluted,
costly
and full of thieves.

In other words, an accurate representation
of 'love' or the pursuit of it – these days.

I walked right up to the Eiffel Tower
and felt as though it were a mirage.
Not as big as I'd imagined.
The marketing seemingly more real –

a couple falls into one another's faces.

Do we even remember what we're looking for? Or is that entirely the point?

The day before, I questioned
how I could (hope)

to run into lovely strangers looking my best
while insisting one would take me
in my most unfiltered form.

Still – the next day – I straightened my hair,
put on my advertisements,
only to mask myself in a book
upstairs Shakespeare and Company.

There, my heart began palpitating
for reasons I was yet to understand –
as if it were running ahead of me, asking me to follow.
Notre Dame glared through the window
as if aware of my future sins.

I began, unsteady to the stairs,
face muddied by sweat
humidity humbling my hair.

Hafiz lines painted on each step

"I wish I could show you..."

***

When I made it – haphazardly – into the bookstore cafe
my eyes were rolling back – words slurring
like the liquid I was in need of.

I slumped into the nearest seat
after barrister, who smelt of croissants
but spoke with an Irish lilt,
passed me a drink.

I was enraptured with him
almost as fast as my vision unblurred.

And as he began closing the store,
he asked me to a bar.
I guess some things don't change –
Men and beer.
Men and a damsel in distress.
But what *was* different...
Me; weak in the knees
for perhaps, more than
the heatstroke
and also – me – early for once.

Galway Bar,
I read him the first part of this poem.
He put earphones in my ears – a song he'd written.
I strained for a beat, a word
the pub's musician wasn't blaring over –

surrendered; gave him back his phone
which appeared to be seven years deteriorated

only to reach him, through Télégraphe.

***

Aspiring Tumbleweed,
you ruffle my hair like T.V. static putting me to sleep.
I finally let go of the words

and insist on your white noise instead;
the losing of composure.

We are all delectable shoulders and biomechanical mishaps.
A guttural ecstasy roseates in your chest,
evading from your throat.
Though, your kisses sound more like morning birds
we never woke to.

In two days, our hands will knock together
as we zip-up my stubborn bag.

At the train station, you'll tell me the difference between Irish and Australian goodbyes.
How where I'm from, they often drag-on until they become hellos again.

You're right, but I'll attempt to conceal the extent of it.

Keep my rucksack on as we hug goodbye.
Keep our final kiss to seconds.
Try not to think about how I will never see you again...
until after I'm on the train.
Or if it's normal for casual dates to kiss you on the forehead
more than the neck.
I'll replay your last words, after your grip slips from mine –
as you stumble over your words,
"see you soon" before correcting yourself.

How I will hope this isn't an accident, but a precursor.
Fate snitching on itself, as it does.

If there are only two choices in life,
love or fear?
I will wonder what a flight back to you is?
Where the urge comes from –
a glimpse of love
or a fear of never knowing?

I hold these small pieces of you
and sometimes I think they are the most significant.
Rarities; the slickest to slip away.

I never did hear your song, but I witnessed
the way you stand in an empty kitchen.
I know you detest hot chocolate as much as I do,

that the paint job on your ceiling, above your bed, is uneven
and you will never unsee it.

I know, you aren't afraid of boredom,
which is to say you aren't afraid of your own mortality.
I know the guitar, leaning up against your wall,
cost more than your car –
which is to say, you have your values in order.

You're most desirable, digitally detached
so, I'll leave you in another country. On a different SIM.

(The city of) love is crowded,
fashionable,
polluted,
costly
and full of thieves
but

I could never claim to be robbed.

ARE YOU AFRAID OR COMFORTED?

I'm convinced I see more
in through your eyes,
than you see out of them.

LANDSCRAPES

M.B. / 2023

You were quite the sight,
and I made quite the scene.

Being with you was a welcome catastrophe;

land*slide*, land*scrape*, land*mark*
of my memory.

You unpin me.
I drop off your map.

But my dimple remains
in the 19th arrondissement.

POETRY AS A TOUCHSTONE

2023

It is well-known, a great number of artists die
never witnessing a world which has witnessed them.

But how many muses die never knowing they were a muse?

The fortunate creators may have had the heart
to share their muse with the world...

but not the bravery

to ask the single individual to
switch on the radio,
drop into the gallery or
pick up the literary journal.

My dear, I'm afraid you are one of those muses

and I am selfish
to put your judgement before your credit.

Would you think I value you more as a product than a presence?

It is not true.

I simply can't bear for you to see
my neural nakedness
– since you.

Besides, the muses never stay,
they are much too wild
and unstable
(this is, of course, the essence of a good muse).

And the ones who would stay
because they are secure and beautiful
and altogether too boring.
Eventually, they leave too
because we don't write poetry about them.

How I'd like you to be the third type

of lover a writer has,

but I'm afraid they're fool's gold –
pyrite every time.

I LIKE YOU

G.P. / 2024

Today, I'm watching a girl do a handstand
in the exact place
we first kissed.

Thinking, how quickly things can turn
upside-down;

all the ways my insecurities
could get the best of us.

I'm trying so hard
not to mess this one up
but I have a tendency to internalise;
broke up with you in my head, ten times last night.

What I mean is, I like you.
I like you a lot.

I like how you wear your late father's wristwatch,
how *only one* of your hands react to the dish soap
but you keep using it because your mother does.

I like the odd streaks of grey hair on the back of your head,
the round New Yorker glasses you slip on
when you get out of bed.
I like your night sweat
even if it makes me lose rest.
Don't care about your morning breath.
I like how you always insist on leaving by 10am
but are still here come two o'clock.

I like the way you kiss more with your mouth, than tongue.
And I'd be disheartened if the mention of Chester Bennington *didn't* have
you tear up.

I think your name is becoming my new favourite word –
a single syllable that windchimes around my mind.

I could go on,
try to keep my head in the clouds,

but I'm an acrobat by design;
tightrope walking   on my palm-lines
– signs I refuse to read –
because the constellations of this concussion
might just be the message I need.

What I'm saying is please,
please, don't let me down
slowly.

Take this messed-up rhythm and rhyme scheme;
everything that tells you I'm unsure.

Make me mean it more.

PUNCTUAL HEARTS
2016

We don’t have punctual hearts;

the beats are   never timed.

Irregular, when we’re apart

but you can never be mine.

We don’t have punctual hearts.

Mine’s still a beat behind.

You’ve taken my breath a f a r

and you’re not the returning kind.

YOUR FAITH IS A NEEDLE

G.P. / 2024

You say there is a stitch
in your stomach

and I wish you knew all my intentions
are honest.

Though, I'm aware the more I try to prove that,
the less genuine I'll appear.

I want to tell you, I'd never break your heart.

Though I want you to tell me,
if I did – I'd be the most devastating one
to watch walk away.

How might we know
who is stringing who along?
With both our guards up...   we won't.
And imagine that is the real threat. Not each other.

I can see you
tiptoeing around me too.
And I don't know how to tell you
to just stomp.
                    Just jump.

Because if you do,
you'll see I'm sincerely a haystack;
ready to catch you.

But your faith is a needle – lost in me.
Sharp. Small.
And so hard to find.

There is a stitch

in both our stomachs,
can we hope a little longer –
it's something threading us together.

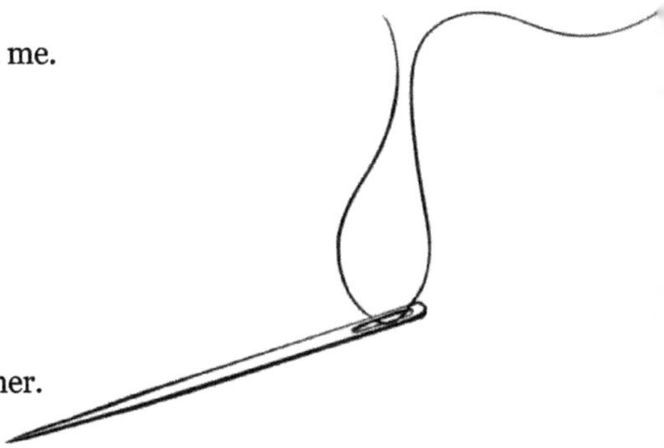

ALL OR NOTHING

2021

I was ‘nothing more’

and you were ‘everything but’;

a perfect fit though at odds.

CHEMISTRY

2017

We press our bodies together,
forcing separate atoms to form one
of a new breed

but it will never be achieved;
we don't bond
just periodically breathe.

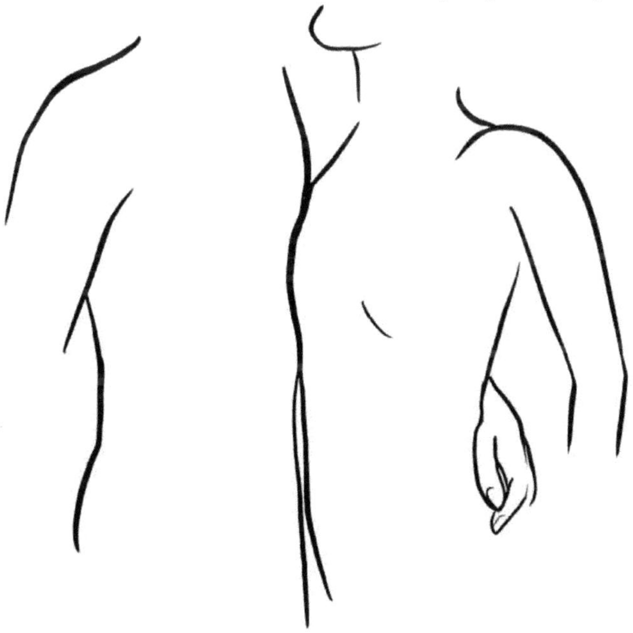

FIRE AND ICE

T.J.V. / 2021

You wrote a love song to cigarettes;
branded
with the gaps between every inhale.

And maybe we burnt out,
because I never knew how much
I'd miss the taste of ash, until now.

You must know what that's like;
caught the scent of *fire and ice*
from an unknown passer-by
and felt a muffled desire...

but everyone has to wake from the dream eventually
and despite all the questions we asked
about the possibility of us,
it never made us lucid enough to last.

THE ONE

Maybe we could have
found '*the one*' in each other...
but in your rating system, 10's are the prize.
I have dyscalculia, though
I don't think the maths works
despite.

Does it matter? When all we are
is a paradox,
Remind me how to forget
nothing but your everything
to me.

CHARR M
2016

You are chained to my heart
don't run or tug too hard.
I couldn't survive a transplant

my insides are too charred
to host one more arsonist
that will burn themself
in a surrogate home.

COMMON DECENCY

T.J.V. / 2021

I know the thought of me causes
a circuit break in your mind.

I would curse you every time you called me sweet,
knowing common decency would have us leave.

Said “Hail Satan” every time you sneezed;
we’d blessed each other
for too many smaller reasons.

You’d say, my teeth glint through my eyes
and my heart, through my smile

or something to that affect.
Challenging.

Maintaining respect in our jest, quick wit,
cute side-eyed arguments.

I don’t want your love or more of your life.
But tell me,
if *‘leaving wasn’t part of the plan’*,
what was it then?

Common decency doesn’t mean much
when there was nothing common about us.

IN VAIN

2015

Is it vain to love a perfect person?
Stupid to let it hurt you?
How about to revive false hope
as often as you butter toast?

My stitches split at every sighting of her face.
No more, no less than yesterday.
The thought of her is a weapon –
afflicting and stemming the blood, at once.

I don't think you understand.
I can't frown;
no one falls in love with someone who is sad.
Certainly not for the second time around.
But my only reason to smile
has left me and let me
down.

Fractured

RELATIONSHIP STAIRCASE

2016

When I saw you I froze.					
Will	*you* stick by my side?				
You	*make*	**nights** come alive.			
Leave	*me*	**only**	*when* you have to.		
Me	*sick*	**with**	*kisses.*	**Another?**	
Alone,	*inside.*	**fights**	*are few,*	**love**	**?**

Read left to right and then top to bottom

DRIVE-THROUGH

P.S. / 2015

I feel like one of those girls
at a drive-thru,
"Hey, can I take your order?"
Then you leave in a few –
I don't know how you changed from
someone who cared to someone who can't.
They say those things don't happen overnight
yet here I am; proof fast food
is less disposable than my heart.

LIFE AFTER YOU

2022

I grieved and then,
worked diligently
to start my life again.

But when does living
after you,
stop feeling like a distraction?
A falsity.

Does it ever?

TO FALL FOR A MUSICIAN

P.S. / 2015

You played that guitar a different way,
pulled my strings and broke me
centre stage.
I knew those chords weren't meant for me
but the sound subdued suspicions and strung
verses in my head, dreams of composure
by completing some-thing, some-one else.

Maybe I'll never be a duet but I thank you
for playing me like one of your instruments.
Heartbreak makes for good lyrics
even though you, me and the melody
are out of sync.

THE STEREOTYPE

2024

You don't have to tell me;
he's an occasional Safe
with too many combinations.

A musician will always say,
he wants to keep it casual
and hence, make a casualty out of me.

He will lose little in closure;
he won't drop his mic or sledgehammer his guitar.
He will tell me all so delicately;

this morning, I found a guitar pick
fallen on my bedroom floor.

DECEMBER
2015

December,
my heart broke witnessing yours
in somebody else's chest.
You were just an illusion
of a place I thought I could rest.

INTELLECTUALISING

2021

Sometimes I question my ability to love
am I just going through the actions;
feeling empathy but not attraction?

No, that can't be true,
there is nothing *this* intense
to take from you.

I can feel the jealousy
I can feel my spirit break
but beyond this mistake, there is no warmth
only distain.

Even so, I don't let go.
Mirage or love?

No one else has ever made me feel
anything so strong
so I like to believe the second one.

For how does one clutch
so staunchly to air,
something that was never really there?

THE NEXT GIRL

2021

The next girl

will be prettier than me
she will have to be;
no one cares as much as I do,
no one could sacrifice as much as I did for you,
no one is as loyal as I was.
Why isn't this your loss?

Maybe your love will be superficial
but to you, depth isn't crucial.
So, you will be happy with

the next girl.

You will give her more;
maybe the ring of the cheater before.
All the things I deserved
instead of the hurt
she will get for less
because I spent all of my energy teaching you
how to treat someone well.

Effort, love
you will give her what I never got.

I made you her type of man;
brought you to life like Frankenstein

but I didn't make a monster
no, much worse...

I made one human again.

TIME TRAVELING BACK TO US

2022

Today, I am glossy in the gardens
as I observe us – lying under the pines.
My head on your chest,
both our eyelids resigned.
I can almost feel again;
shorter strands of our hair – afloat, like the wisterias –
in the now, stagnant air.

I doubt this surprises you – my time-travel.
You know me so well, it probably seems casual by now;
the way animals magnetise,
how my body shape-shifts; plots my demise.
Needle of clock and the scale synchronised.

You've seen how light bulbs blow
in rooms I stand.
Remember me upon your shoulders – changing one
as if we stood a chance.

You'd think with all these abilities,
I could make *ends* meet,
if there are two loose strings,
wouldn't you tie them together? ...well I did.

Alas, you're loose and I'm lost.
Those are two different things;
they do not make a knot.

At best, a paradox;
forever bound, from our separation
or bound to fall apart when too close
and I can't tighten the cords
or break them – if it were a choice.

To tell the truth,
another light bulb has blown.
I'm not tall enough to reach it on my own
and I don't know anything about building
a home.

But that moment was one. A home.
And we were the greatest architects.
I could live in it forever,
not one regret.

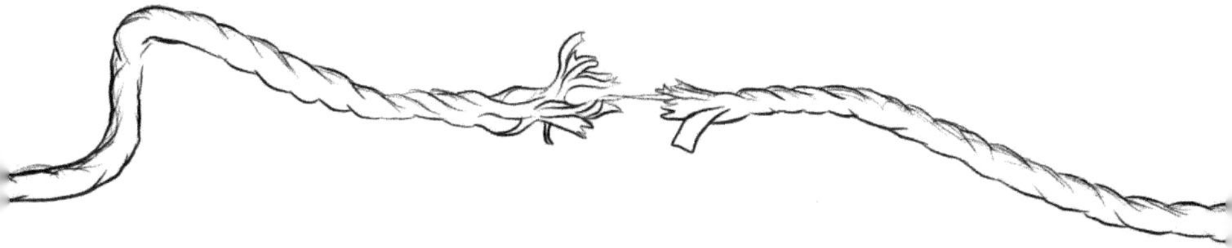

POSTAL STAMPS

The message you left
– needless of paper or ink –
envelopes me,
in a way you never will
again.

'Newcastle'

...placed strategically
in the corner.

Far from my address,
that no longer feels central;
or a focal point.

Most of me knows, distance is irrelevant
to the real space between us.
But what good is *most*?

If a surgeon informed you there's a 90% chance you'll live,
admit you'd still be thinking about the other 10%.

I don't know which I'm more afraid of.

All I know is, a scalpel
can feel more like a letter opener

and this time, you won't be here if I wake up.

When they place the mask over my mouth,
I count backwards
in 25c intervals

rewinding back to when
postal stamps hadn't been replaced by timestamps.

I'm numb before I've calculated
how many of either it would take,
to send you back to me
or to realise,

I never had *enough*.

You know, I could never have enough.

DESOLATE
2015

Melancholy;
melt in lands
unholy
in an abyss of

Harm suppressed;
between two palms pressed
together.
Remind us we are

Desolate;
descending to a
solitary fate
where days

Gloomy;
glue me
to my memories
cold cruelty and

Shame;
an attempt at shadowing
the untamed.

UNDERSTUDIES

2024

When my dates brush their hands over the cat we raised together,
I can't help but feel a flash in my temple
and something winding in my throat.
How do I say, I'm watching my memories
being taped over before me?

Life tells me to keep rolling
and I think of a steep hillside.
I want to scream "Cut. Cut. Cut.";
I want to call every new vignette what it is.

How do I tell them?
Absence is the truest understudy of reminiscence.

It is all I know myself to be;
the binding of retro reels –
film so flammable it catches
each time I turn up
the exposure.

TINA LOUISE

2024

I was brought-up on black-and-white pictures, 60's cinema.
The series that soothed me so, a since-realised tea party with ghosts.
Three of the cast – dead, a decade before I was born.
Now all of them, apart from one.

The beautiful Ginger Grant;
such a sleek young thing, Hollywood jewel.
Could have anyone she wanted or so I assumed.

I beheld her then,   scant though enamoured –
her marauding figure, satin skin,
tug of her top lip as she spoke.

Foresaw myself – forsaken.

Now I'm grown, reading that the actress is so much more –
resolute, reasonable
and I can't help but think...   lonely too.

Who could bare being the final fading link?
Don't dream tonight –

keep counting
her daughter, her grandchildren – do, but when you read:
at 89, she is still hoping to find love,

decline the outer corners of your eyes and soften –

resign futile periphery.

Rename her home
'The City That Slept On Her'.

CANDLELIT DINNERS
2016

She was a candle you lit up
to burn down,
to smell the chaos sweet,
to calm your corrupt mind.

Brilliant flame, too
bright for her own good.
Ruined with hope that you
would change.
At the least, put her out
before she evaporated
of her own fervour.

Oh, how she beamed
at those candlelit dinners,
if only she'd have known:
it was all a rouse
for you to steal her light.

THIN ICE

2017

You polish your ‘prize’ with black and blue.
Fill your cup with crimson undue.

You say she wouldn’t know what love was
if it hit her in the face
and with that,

she holds a fragment
of ‘thin ice’ to the skin
you stained.

EGGSHELLS

2022

He had a specific way of shopping for partners;

he picked her

like a lock.
Then contained her within her own insecurity;

trauma (bonds)
you break it
you buy it.

but she, as an *object*,
was the only one who paid.

Aware no one keeps anything they've broken
in their home for long
and worse still, does not care to handle
it carefully anymore...

eggshells crush her feet.

Will he spill his yoke on another
before she is released?

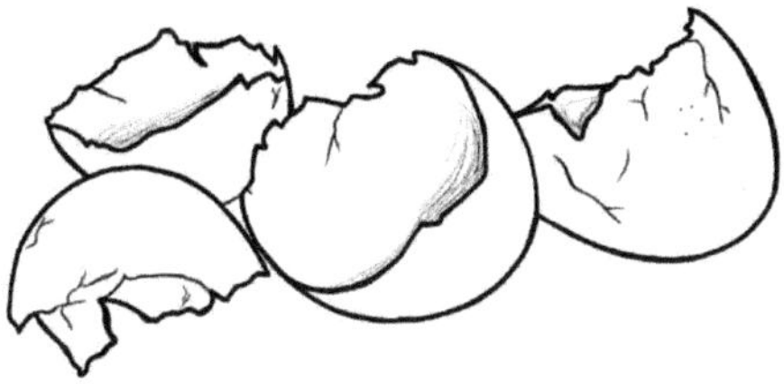

LOSING A FRIEND

2017

We used to be linked, knew exactly
how each other would think.
I wonder if now,
you have a sense of my grief
or if you're serenely un-synched.
May it be the last, for it is
a better reason for us
to be apart.

LUCY

2022

I was there
holding you
as you departed but

last night I opened the back door
and in the silence, I braced myself
for your scuffle of paws
as you'd normally rush up to me.

As I slept on the couch, this morning,
I swear I felt your wet nose nudge my knee,
your wagging tail, sway your whole body
and the floor beneath.

It's those transitional places that get me;
where I can no longer pretend you are
simply outside if you are not in

or inside when I'm out.
When I am half-waking and half ghost,
I forget you – my dear friend – left this earth
some time ago.

There are some types of heaviness
only more weight upon you, may lift
such as your canine's head on your stomach.

MEMORIES

2021

How could I

lose the memory of you

without losing some of my mind

and heart

with it too?

III
2015

"I loved you".
His words lost
in a breeze
like she was,
but only,
only a
hurricane.
Those few words
she had left
were past tense,
as was he,
when she went.

There he stood,
lost in all.
found by cries,
bound by her
memory
but never
by her arms.

Here darkness
swells so sweet.
All around,
underneath,
like oceans
to swallow
all his grief
and above,
lightning streaks.

It took three.
Three steps to,
to escape
off the edge.
Three words to
destruct him,
all he was.
One breath to
be taken.
Fractured by
time, as he...
he whispered
"Goodbye".

LAWS OF FRICTION

2016

Hand in hand,
I felt like I was suspended over a bridge.
I know I'd been weighing you down
but all you had to do was lift.

Alas, the laws of friction remained the same;
for one to move on, the other must fall away.

At impact, you thought I wouldn't feel a thing.
How could I? It was solid concrete.

No heartbeat for me.
No problems for you.
A painless death, for two.

X

There was a time
I felt like treasure
when you kissed me.

Never recognising
the *X marking the spot*

as a symbol
for an unknown
replacement

and soon to be a name,
you refer to me by.

DIRTY HANDS

Why did you dig your hands into my chest
and rip out my heart if you couldn't hold onto it;
if you knew you couldn't deal with this bloody mess?

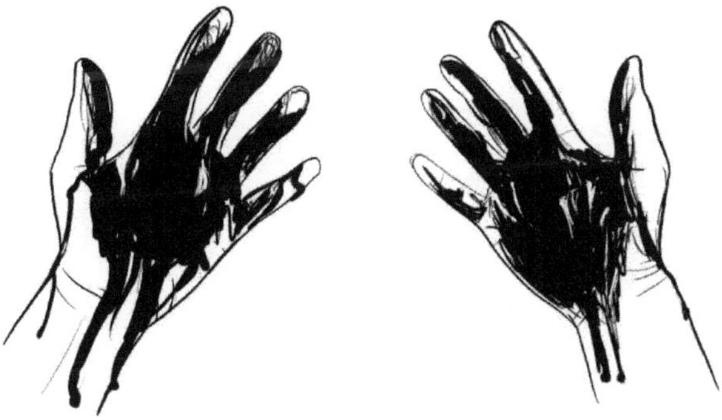

USELESS RICHES

2020

You have so much to give
even your damaged,
worn down to the bone affections
are more than most people can comprehend.

While you know,
it's not your full capacity – that disappeared long ago –
they don't;
they believe you overflow.

I'm not calling them unobservant or naïve
or suggesting you have some superiority,
I'm saying:

Quit while you're ahead – people don't pay their debts.

Love is a currency that will run you broke
in a world so corrupt but reaching for it all at once.
The more you have within you,
the more hands upon your chest.
I'm sorry you know what it's like
being an atm.

BACKSTABBED
2021

I never turn on anyone
and no one has my back
so how is it,
I harbour so many
stab wounds there?

SHRAPNEL
2021

When I said to leave me alone,
I meant stop touching me
with your hands of destruction
and hold me
with the safety I know you have within you;

hold together the pieces of me, you

f r a g m e n t e   d.

AXLE

2024

I could say,
you only cross my mind for mere minutes
but there is a playlist with your initials on it,
10hrs long.

I could say,
I've moved on
but this is going to take more than a change of cities.

If you must know,
I have been on dates but

I don't have my foot in any door,
because I'm too busy
keeping my fingernails in yours.

Not that we've spoken in a year.
I've learnt my sentiment is a bad omen
and my mind, a prize-winning ox.

So maybe it doesn't count for a lot –
to say,
I miss sleeping on your chest.
To say
I love you to pieces.

When
    'I love you to pieces'
    means 'you love me...

    (into) pieces'.

PERMANENT

2023

When the tattoo-artist was doing your sleeve,
they worked around a fast-fading scab –

You were supposed to come back;
fill in the blank
but you took a fondness to the emptiness.
Created a story from it.

There is a permanent vacant space
in me too.

Although, I still wince when it's touched

or when I think about how many more tattoos
you've put on your body since.
Ones I have not committed to memory.

I still can't untangle my head
from the Celtic knots upon your chest,
all the ink there – has bled

over me.

You must be over me. By now.
Just as I think, I could make peace with our history:
you would've acquired a new one.

The buzz of our moments marked me,
a purity enclosed by immortal grey.

We are just as bad as each other,
when it comes to

turning a scratch into a scar.

1000 NIGHTS OF SOLITUDE

2024

You could say, my love life is eventful –
when you read all those poems.

It's true, I haven't been alone *every* night
within the past three years
but I have spent 1081 nights alone in that time
and it's beginning to feel like the same thing.

You see, I tend to stretch out sparse nights
or the dream of them
so it appears, each year – I have more than one...
one.... less-than-a-lover.

Usually they're travellers,
the emotionally unavailable or star-crossed.
In other words, anyone who 'could' love me
but has better excuses not to.

Otherwise, I've been told I am like drowning.
All-consuming the second you let me through your lips.
I'm vodka disguised in a water bottle;

so, these days, I stick to tossing breadcrumbs –

    not to retrace my steps back
    like Hansel and Gretel

    or to lure
    people with a pigeon appetite,

    but because maybe I won't notice it this time;
    if my heart dissipates bit-by-bit.

I said, I toss breadcrumbs.
I toss pebbles at the wrong windows.

    Because I thought it was safer.
    I was lied-to about predators;

    told they're strictly carnivorous (no glutton for gluten),
    that only big rocks provoke big beasts.

After all, it feels pathetic to say
I'm still attached to permanence.
I know it's hopeless, I know it's dated
I know it's everything women have been bred to want.
A sorry expectation.

Maybe even selfish, as the person I am now;
allowing myself to feel

but only if I blend in; move towards
the opposing mood – be a gradient.

Where I learn, friends aren't the same
and I could buy myself roses
but it's only ever a small scent of sentiment.

I'm beyond touch-starved –
I'm touch-shrivelled,
touch-deceased,
touch-six feet under.

And I've tried short term relationships
because...
What right do I have to feel lonely,
when there are a multitude of people, asking to be let in?
Who am I to be a beggar and chooser?
When does patience become denial?

Is no one good enough for me?
Is everyone too good for me?
Is that my version of bisexuality?

I mean, you'd think that would increase my chances at least.

You must know, I don't always feel this way.
Perhaps, it's only today.
Perhaps, it's only after reading romance books.
Or only when I'm not reading.
Perhaps, it's only a feeling
or perhaps, it's *the* only feeling
awaiting me.

"You're young" they reassure
and I wince at the fact, *this* is my prime,

while I reply, 'yeah guess I am a catch-   *22.*'

Because I want to be 'Your Honour', not your Judge.
Because I want to be courted with no 'order'.
But it doesn't work, when I'm the only one who's *'got time'*.

Shall I tell you about today?
That I knew he wouldn't show – again.
When the waiter asked, I replied 'a table for one'
because what changed?
Apart from that this time, I didn't get a look of pity
after sitting there for an hour.

When you've been single this long, you begin to notice:
there are a set of questions you ask yourself every time you shave,
there are too many things sold in sets
and coffee shops don't arrange tables for one.

I don't know how to talk without going deep,
been told solitude has a similar effect on my thoughts to LSD
and I pick-up all these hobbies
to fill the time
and to reaffirm I'm interesting.
But I only feel like E.T. –
so removed, remembering isolation breeds.

I mean yeah, I'm fine
as long as you stop reminding me
it's all a matter of time.

SINKING IN YOUR FOOTSTEPS

P.S. / 2017

Thinking you could give me direction;
what more of a mistake?
You trod in deep water
to suppress your shallowness
and I sunk in your footsteps,
denying my fate.

Deep, sandy sinkholes
seduced us side by side.
I drowned under the surface
but you didn't.
You are taller than I.

Please tell me this isn't my last breath,
please tell me this isn't my last step.
I don't want to die in the shadow
of something I couldn't get.

I want to walk on virgin sands
never claimed by feet like yours,
that stomp me down for esurient shores.

SIX FEET

2017

You always kept at least six feet

away from me.

Now, I'm beginning to understand why.

FUNERAL

2021

It's not like you'd appear at my funeral
but I would still die for you.

It would be this thought
that killed me,
alone.

When situation never arose,
I subconsciously made it so;
every living moment – dying
in wake of the past ones
we shared.

DROP-TAIL

2021

Like a skink drops its tail
– for a second chance at life –
you've dropped your expectations and boundaries
for relationships to survive.
And you thought that meant
only part of you would die.

WHAT NEVER BEGAN
2018

There's no way to argue with their departure if they never vowed to stay. Relationship courtesy doesn't apply to friendships; cheating is no more than a feeling but clingy has much to pay.

Left with your illusory realities, imagined arguments and fictional reasons why your North is their South. You may wonder if you're to blame for the increased distance between you. If interfering with them leaving, only repels them further.

The fastest way to learn you're a magnet, honey,
is by turning the other way.

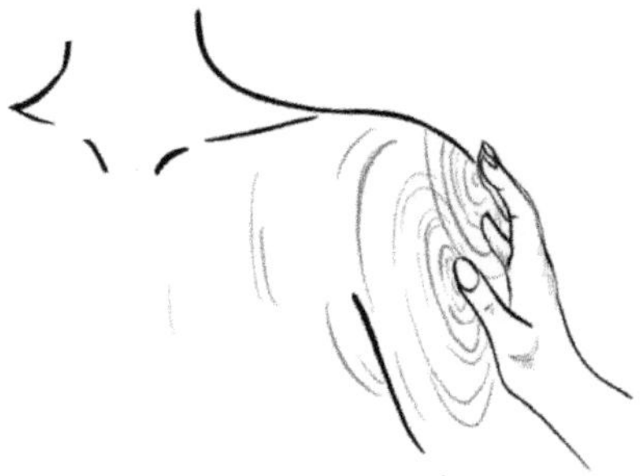

PEOPLE WATCHING

2023

Outside the Intercontinental
her fingers are interlaced with his,
but his fall slack
as if they're holding nothing at all.
Her strides are unbalanced;
she angles into his shoulder, smiling up at him.
He keeps an even pace.

They continue walking
and walking and walking
and he never curls those loose fingers
over her knuckles.
She never seems to question why.
They both seem unphased – at best distracted in conversation.

Only I feel the loneliness of her hands.

This image follows me home,
I squeeze my own palms together.
Observe,
if one hand squeezes too tightly,
the fingers of the other rebound,
as if a reflex test.
And
if both hands do not meet in synchronicity,
the first to squeeze
will slant the architecture of affection.

This is how I rationalise it away...

Rationalise the rations those men threw
becoming the best they could do.
Rationalise until she becomes the problem
for holding on.

Rationalise until she remains 'she'
not me.
Remember, I must not remember

she is not me.

Fighting

NO PROMISES

I don't make promises anymore
not because I can't keep them
but because I do,
too long after
the reasons have left the room.

AS WITHIN, SO WITHOUT

2023

Even though you know most eggs are good,
you test them every time.

Drop them
in a vessel of water, see if any float –
your 'swimming of witches' defence mechanism.

Maybe it's a waste of time, as some say,
though you prefer it, to one day dealing with a mess
of what wasn't meant for you.

Imagine fishing that spoiled sun out of its own vapour;
how delicately you must despise it.
Wondering, which is the least lethal way to breathe
and where is the most forgiving place
for you to elude it.

Maybe you'll never make it in this life –
as a poet or lover.
But the good eggs always sink.

GUILTY

2017

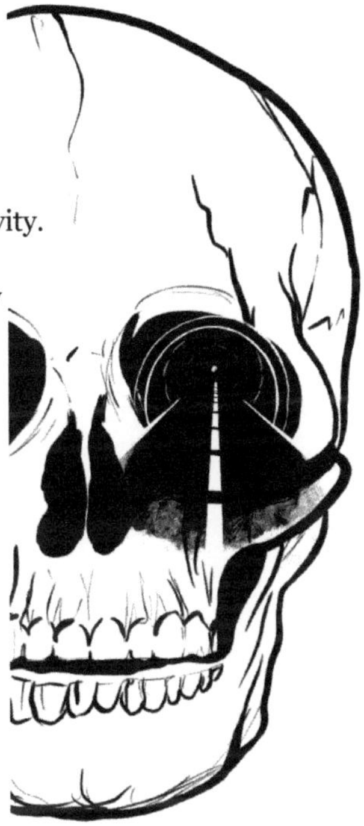

Abjure your thoughts about me,
let them evaporate premature,
flee from them as they reverberate
down tunnels unheard.
Caught in coils and brain circuits,
a toiled mess it seems, derailed from sensitivity.
Please, please, please
whisper once again, about how we were only
wed in whimpers and circumstance.
Skull interior decorated with
unfamiliar family pictures.
Riveted with foreseen screams.
It's better this way,
to slice our salvaged association.
Ha, yes – I'll plead guilty for your faults
if only, for the protection of imprisonment.
We'll both be safer that way
with excuses for why we started something
we knew would never last.

THE CRASH

2017

I am the bullets of rain on your windscreen,
clouding your view.
I am the vengeful rubble you roll over,
piercing your wheels.

But the toxic gas;
the leaking fuel that nurtured the fire...
that was you.

Pick up the remnants of our crash
hold them in your arms
and wait for the flashbacks.

I am in everything you see,
everything you breathe

because I left a part of me behind.
Where else could it be?

ARCADE

2021

Expected me to be
a token to you; transactional
and taken on my aesthetic but

it wasn't about my worth
more than your actions.

TRANSPARENCY

2021

Being transparent
never meant cheapening
or being as breakable
as glass.

GHOST

2021

It’s ironic really,
you’re afraid of death
yet you moved that planchette
to ‘Goodbye’ in the way you left.

Never mind, my lachrymose.

If you want to ghost,
I’ve got smoke and salt.
I don’t beg, I banish.

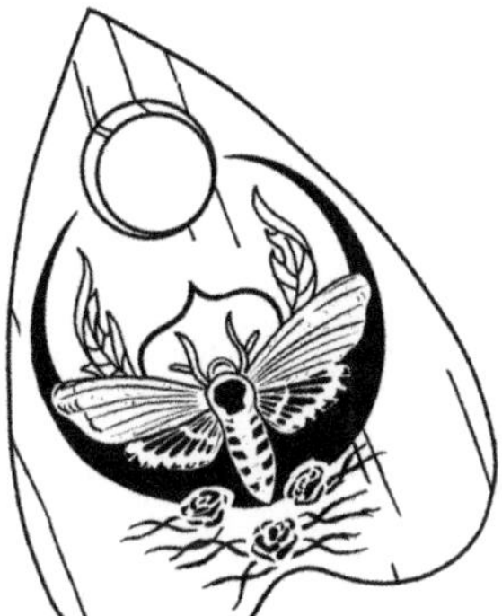

AN ABANDONED LIBRARY
2022

She came composed
of more metaphors than molecules.

You misinterpreted her
highlighted words
as you shut the door behind her,

and did not leave the key in;
no page marked –

reserved
your visions
but not the space for them.

I ask you,

who can write in a closed book?

WATER CYCLE

2022

Be wary of the ones
soft as clouds,
they hold lightning
and the little they say, resounds.

If you are inconsistent
she will even the grounds.
Releasing is her power
to protect;
reiterating boundaries
between your lows and her depths.

She did not learn to float
and host angels
by allowing mortals to drag her down.
You can't drown that which becomes oceans
or burn that which rises above mountains.

She is not something you could ever hope to possess.
Drink her in
she passes through your skin.
Feel her mist in your eyes
but know you are not missed yourself.

People like her, have made an art of coming apart.
Pain; the deliverance beyond plane or prophet.

NARCISSIST

You better lubricate your fabrications
because I no longer pride myself
on swallowing your pride for you.

It's like swords down my throat,
without the applause.
I don't want to
never be remembered
as someone without a voice.

I stop internalising your projections and
in doing so,
arm myself

with lengthened understanding
of what wounded me.
Understanding no longer with – or due to – sympathy.

Not your sheath.
Silver will always look better
on than *in* me.

EAGLE
2015

You only ever cry
like an eagle;

in search of prey.

YOU GREW (OUT) OF ME

You grew (out) of me
and you think that means
you're in my head
but boy you're only in my hair.

STEALING LIGHT

Fetishized with fury,
easier with ash.

You reach into the pits
of women,

knowing not what you want
or already have.

You think you scorch them to their core but
you merely stoke the dragon within them.

Take their crunchy honeycomb –
almost edible.
If not for their light.
If not for their potency.

And once again, you must be taught
what sings within us
singes too.

POISONOUS

People would call me 'Snow White'
then, 'That Witch'
but now, I realise I'm more like the apple;
sweet until you bit in.

ROUTINE CLEANING
2022

Treat me like a chore,

I'll clean myself

of you.

STRENGTH

2022

Strength is one of few things
that can be taught by those most
inexperienced and ignorant, of it.

– *You taught me but I am the master.*

BURIAL

2019

Treating me like dirt
will not ground you
and there will come a time when
what you stepped on
will instate your burial.

I'm a simple rule of nature;
don't jump into deep water if you can't swim.

I'm a simple rule of nature;
don't provoke it and it will have no reason to harm you.

I'm a simple rule of nature;
don't wait until sundown to think of shelter.

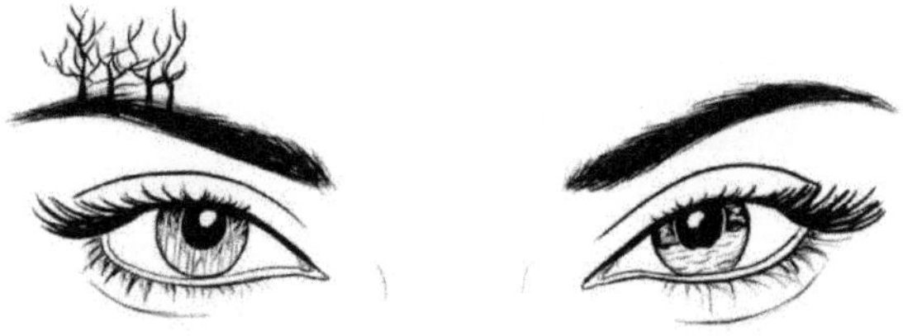

So they don't. They just *don't* with me.

ARTEFACT

2019

They used you in every conceivable way,
so why do you still feel so wasted?

How can they possess you?
When they don't carry with them.
Not a single shred

of consideration for you.

I wish you knew,
your purpose does not revolve around
being the purpose of someone else.

You're a lost artefact
no one knows the value of yet
and there is strength in that.

One day, I believe you will remember
without having to remind yourself:

they never owned you and
you never owed yourself to any of them.

NOT ONE IN A MILLION

2020

You are NOT 'one in a million'.

If that's what they told you,
along with 'I can't get enough of you'.

For that is to say there are at least
8, 000 other 'ones' out there.

(Population Earth: 8 billion)

A weak loophole they used to move onto the next one
without establishing where you ended.

EVOLVING EMPATH

2022

I refuse to be tender,
like a bruise.

But I could possibly be warm
as is a fire
when it too, is fed.

GIVER

2021

We learnt; it's not love
if given with expectation

and in doing-so forgot
we are worth reciprocation.

MORE THAN A FIGURE OF SPEECH

2021

I know there are many types of love out there,
all valid,
but what is it *you* require?

Maybe what they said was true, maybe they did love you with their whole heart.

But there is a difference between loving someone with your whole heart and loving them with your whole being.

Have you ever recognised this,
in your body refusing closeness to anyone but them?
In your energy and emotions being entangled in theirs?
In your mind considering the best ways to put a smile on their face?

Even after you lose them,
your spirit refusing to let hope die, though you may will it, so many times.
Your eyes searching for them in the most unlikely places.
And when you do, physically, let them go,
as it may be the most tender thing you could ever do.
You never let them go thinking they are unlovable, unwanted or unworthy;
respecting them with *their whole being* too.

So, if they said
they gave you their whole heart
and you believed them
but still felt there was something missing
then maybe you were right.

All their heart may *want* you to be their future
but *all* of *them* would
make sure nothing could stop that from happening.

Explain to me how else your heart so impossibly broken,
still loves so wholly?
And how else their heart given everything it needs to be full,
can be all but empty.

Darling,
you deserve the fierce devotion you so freely give.
So, I ask you again,

did they love you with their whole being?
Or just one of their many organs?

Facing

IF FLOWERS FIXED EVERYTHING

A.B.Y / 2021

Yesterday, I watched a video
of a physicist explaining how to
turn a sphere inside out without it imploding.

I thought about the globe;
the earth between us,

bouquets of buds opening at different times,
the procedure –

how to give,
twist and bend without breaking.

I thought of how we'd tried
to close the distance between us;
bring what's inside to light

but I don't think even a genius
could figure that one out.

I must remind myself:
individually, we are not unlovable
but together, we are unsolvable.

And no matter how many times I rearrange those letters,
the S doesn't fit,
this initial of my surname wants to live.

ENOUGH OF NOT BEING ENOUGH

2019

I think, all you've wanted to hear
is that you're *enough*.
Even if in the past, it's meant acting-out
to catch the word
from a sharp tongue.

NOT ALL BIRDS

2022

Not all birds are made to sing love songs.

Some mimic – lie,
others steal shiny things
and even the wisest owl
knows little of colour
or what resides in the light.

But all of them
keep breathing
more efficiently than any other creature to exist.

Lungs left perpetually open.

Pneumatic;
this hollowness you harbour within your bones
could be your gift too –
to be air-   (borne again).

Hold space – it will hold you.

THIEVES
2021

Thieves only take things of value
so please know;

when you find yourself being used
for that heart of yours,
for your energy.

It is not because you are cheap
like they make you out to be.

They thought they could trick you,
tell you, 'love comes with an expense'.

Switching your '*price tag*'
for theirs –

as if tallying was the devotion,
not the sacrifices
and willingness
to serve.

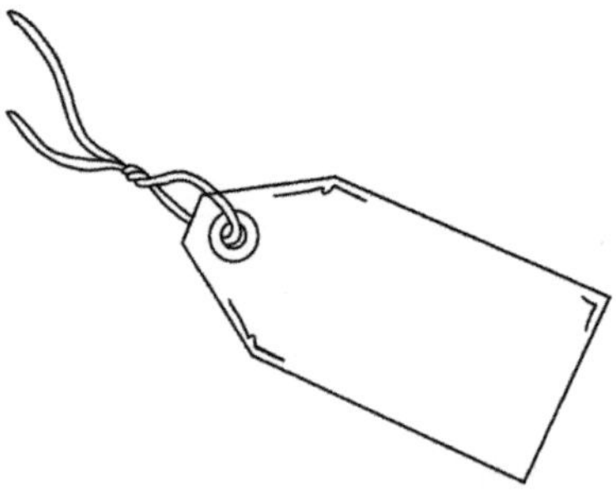

ACCESSIBILITY
2020

Accessibility
will continue to be confused with attraction
to all whom can't comprehend
self-worth being separate to ego.

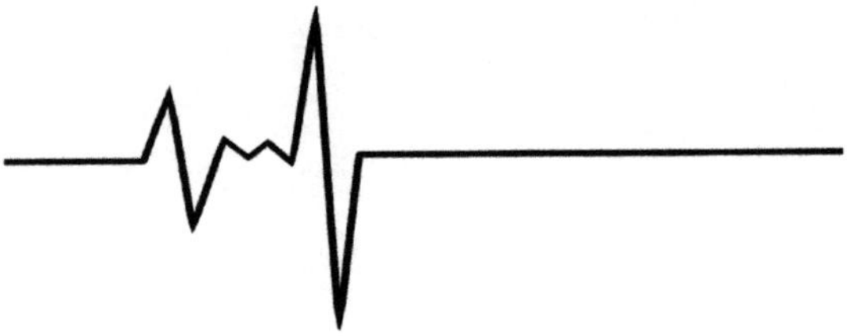

PEOPLE PLEASER

2021

When will you realise? You weren't designed to please
or help
everyone in this world.

If you're lucky your heart will beat 2.5 billion times before death

but there are 8 billion people on this earth.

It is not self-indulgent to live for yourself.

LET TIME TELL SO IT DOESN'T HAVE TO HEAL

2022

Everyone wants a partner who appears
head over heels for them
until they get amnesia from the fall
or call everything they felt an accident.

You hardly need to say, "slow down, wait"
as they barrel your way.
You know you're not the destination anymore
or even the journey –
more like the lane to overtake.

Please consider Time;
the teller of truths,
rather than something to in-debt yourself through.

NEVER ABOUT US

2022

Maybe love was never about us,
but the vibrance we brought
into other people's lives
because of it.

THE DICHOTOMY OF DEPARTURE

2023

Have you ever had your heart broken
by an entire continent?

Have you travelled?
Have you seen-off new jade waves,
stepped into the howl of banshee trains.
Then, caught the topography of gold veined cities
like candle-light upon beaded lace.

And the bagpipes, have you heard those bagpipes?
(ventricles of cobblestone cardiology).

When I tell you, I went to the churches –
rays of purple light rapturing through stained glass,
would you believe I found redemption?
Bent at the knees
                    in street alcoves,
for the accordions, violins
and wretched souls that played them.

Would you believe, I never felt homesickness
like that of my long-buried ancestors – since returning
to the country of my birth;

knowing the privilege it is –
I wake disorientated, at the wrong temperature,
to sounds I'm supposedly familiarised with – young sparrows
fly up into the trees
like autumn leaves falling in reverse.
I am craving contrary seasons.

Don't you know?

The most devastating way to break a heart
is to fill it too much.

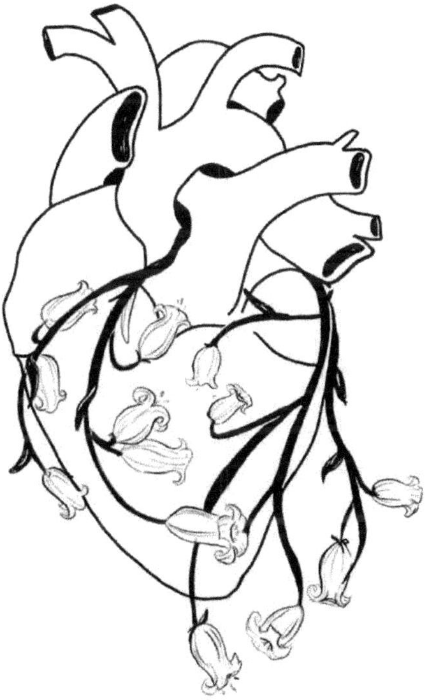

DAUGHTER OF A MARTIAL ARTIST

2023

My father taught me,

'Lead from the (heart) centre'
'Leave no gaps when you hold them'
'Make space – you want to be real close or far away'

What's true in combat translates equally into affection.

So, I'm still learning how to break

my

fall.

CONVERSATIONS ON A DIFFERENT PLANE

2024

I have my father's ears; anti-helix. Piercing
pains after oceanic dives
or when pot is sucked too quickly through the pipe.

They always get blocked driving up hills
and on aeroplanes –
though, I suppose most people's do.

When I was small, there was a time the pressure got so much,
I was deaf for three days after we landed in Perth.

Felt like being trapped inside a radio, or conch shell;
riding the in-between-waves.

Maybe the anonymous frequency *is* a message after all, a warning
we are getting too close to heaven or hell for our age.

But if you chew, swallow and give into a yawn
most problems subside.

At least that's what my father says.

"So, anyway, do you have a stick of gum?...

Yes?

I'm sorry, I can't hear you"

...at least that's what my father says

after he describes sonic booms; the sound barrier
and unfortunate windows that look a bit like you.

THE LANGUAGE OF TREES

2023

The trees gift the wind a gentle whisper; a name to its invisibility.
Thousands of soft leaves, each brushing-up against one another.

You can't pinpoint which specifically,
contribute more to the collective.
By themselves, we'd barely hear anything at all.

Imagine if all the times
we hugged someone we cared about,
collapsed into a moment.

What would that sound like?

Would a hand running up a torso
whisper much differently.

If we heard every punch that landed
on earth
would our ear drums burst?

The trees teach us that touch
is communication – there are messages
in sensations.

Knowledge in the pits of our stomachs.

That the smallest things we do
can create a movement
stronger than we know.

Wind and leaves are not separate,
nor are we from our surroundings.

THE LANGUAGE OF TREES II

2024

You wanted a witness
someone who felt your pain like their own
so you told them everything,
put them outside of time
and themselves;
an entity standing in the corner
of your birth room.

And how could they run?
Embalmed in your life and death.

How close can one reliably witness
before they become a fatality too?
The better part of a backswing.

You must know your pain is never too much
for the earth. For the moon. For whatever your God is.
The way you process doesn't have to be of the axe.

There is a tree in your hometown
which has watched you age,
watched you cry after you fell off your bike,
it saw you on your graduation day
and the way you looked at your first love.
It held your absence
after you moved cities.

Never to abandon.
Never abandoned.
Root systems communicating through soil,
to be the records held in the tree
outside your current home.

Because your vibration will always be the most precise language.
Where what is spoken   is diminished,
any dilution of energy,   tells a story in itself.

If you let this understanding follow you – wherever you go –
you will never have to repeat yourself.

FINAL BOW
2023

The final bow is
part of the performance.

This much, you've observed.

The curtains are veils,
glimpsing at what's nevertheless out-of-reach;
the true character.

If you are to connect these wires again – lift
and be lifted –
it is only with the trust

when all is through,
the two of you will express gratitude
without costumes.

If you hope to take the final bow
it's only in this manner.

The way hands meet isn't scripted;

half-expected but never promised nor bid upon.

CREDITS

2023

Writing has always been sacred;
a place to scream my name without it deafening me.
Purpose housing every stray feeling.

And I'm still trying,
not to lose myself
in my loss.
But sometimes I feel my pulse,

and it's not ink. It is anemia
and oxygen.

We forget our hearts
are more often accredited as metaphors.

As if they're not already doing enough.

Even so, I extend this pen;
all my words   defrauding the very thing
that allows them to be.

All my words
waiting for me   to stray,

to find them
kinaesthetically.

Acknowledgements

I'd like to thank everyone involved in my journey as a poet. Thank you Mum, for putting me through the Davis Dyslexia program and Dad for your consistent support. Thank you Tim for all your guidance over the years when it comes to poetry. Thank you Sam for helping me recover this manuscript after I accidentally deleted it from my computer. Thank you Claire and Analeisha for your most valuable opinions.

And of course, I must give credit to all the people who showed me love or broke my heart, gifting me with something to write about.

About the Author

Danah Slade is a 22-year-old writer, embracing dyslexia as a strength. Her poems have appeared in publications such as 'Australian Poetry Journal', 'Beyond Queer Words Anthology' and 'StylusLit'. She has performed in both the Adelaide and Edinburgh Fringe Festivals. Currently, she resides in Adelaide, South Australia. You can find her either drinking green tea beside her black cat, or fire spinning.

IG: @thepoisonouspoetess
@danahslade

Coming Soon

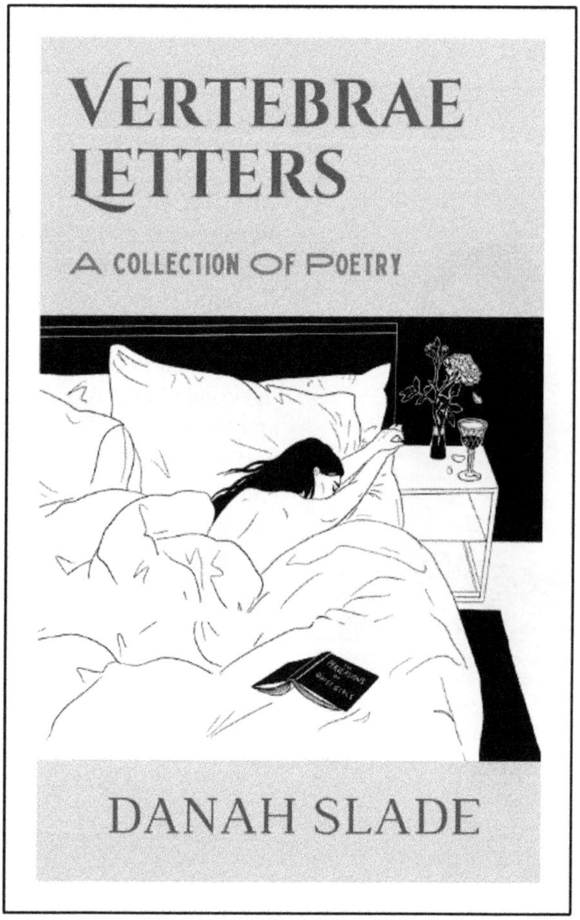

If our bodies could speak to us, what would they say?

Slade channels poetry from her lived experiences with depression, endometriosis, chronic fatigue, derealisation, anxiety and so on. As the collection progresses, poems of humble healing are interwoven into the pages. '*Vertebrae Letters*' highlights the importance of being attuned to our bodies and the environments around us. Poems written from hospital beds transform into subtle insights. From watching rain cascade down concrete steps, to observing insects in the sun, we learn the power of small moments.

C1 Jane Doe

She knows Pain on a first name basis,
but never introduces it;
something that's always with her – talking over
everyone she meets.

The people and events we struggle to speak of
are often those that have made us feel nameless,
ourselves.

S2 Frost Flower

It becomes clear after
you split at the base
feeling nothing but your own frigidity –

how foreign you are.

The birds, the bears, even burrowing worms
(all) have this shared experience, as with your own genus.

But you....
against all your cynical servitude –

vampiric skin ribboned for the taking,
withering away at the first display of warmth.

You cannot make ‘cataclysm’ feel
as beautiful as it sounds.

Though, you *can* make breaking apart *look* lovely,
and be fouler for it.

The mist enamours you,
epitome of both gentle and smothering.

Such is the very lassitude of your longing;
ambiguous, amorphous – twisting into the smallest spaces,
slowing down the busiest streets.

Wanting to be more than a mould inducing
Martian. Martian. Martian of a marshland.

Wanting to be more than a mask.
Wanting to be damp in all the right ways.

Wanting to be someone’s clarity
and seen-through.

First published in ‘StylusLit’

L3 Rain Dance

Concrete stairs turn into water features during heavy rainfall.

Falling down,

taking steps backwards

or crying

could be the most transformative thing you do.

Coming Soon

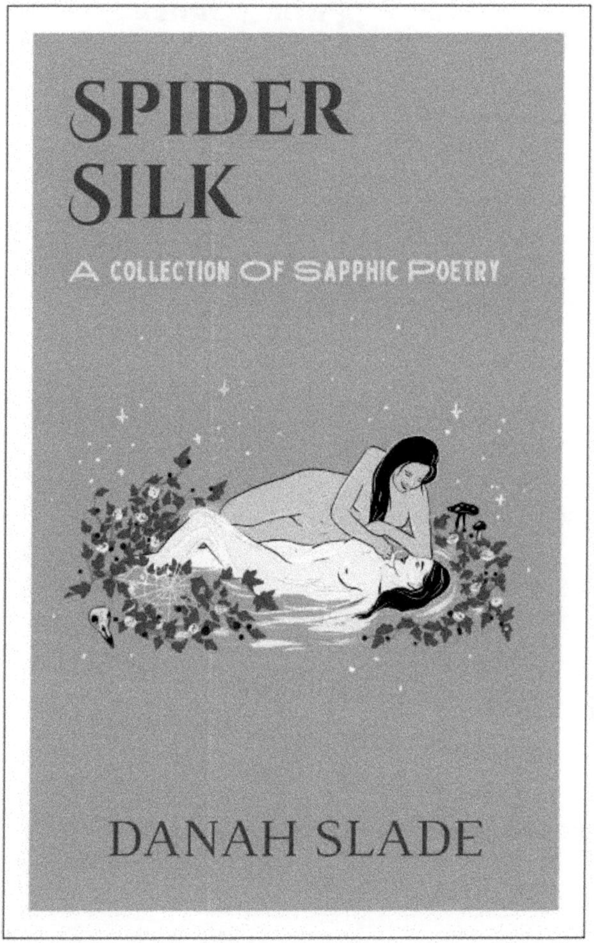

'Spider Silk' is a beautiful nightmare of verses, delving into the sapphic experience through the lens of love and death. The collection demands the idea of queer sexuality being 'unnatural' to be re-examined through a profusion of nature imagery. It speaks to anyone who has experienced internalised homophobia, navigated the queer dating scene, or lost a partner. *Slade* reclaims narratives of historically villainised voices and reframes how we perceive feminine sensuality.

She's the Skeleton in My Closet

Most people fight to keep their love alive,
I labour differently; continuously *nailing* mine in an upright coffin.
I must: preserve her cheeks pale, heart cold and eyes unblinking.
She's the skeleton in my closet.

Foreboding of a confession, forbidden obsession,
every time her name brushes past my lips.
A real kiss might be less obvious.

Secrecy threatens to lessen.
Do I shiver – fearful or invigorated?
It's as if she, I have killed,
'*Come out* with it!', guilt weighs heavy. That,
with Pride, 'Look how I've made her mine'.

They must never discover the vivacity in her bones;
for that is to know my own heart
that beats against them, along with my butterflies
trapped within.

Should they observe how she almost blushes or blinks,
more gaze than glazed-over when she looks at me –
should they know of the *life* I inspire within her;
I would faster claim the title of Murderess.
Taking her out, becomes just that;
a narrative easier for them to digest.

They would faster *tie the knot*, eternal
in our stomachs than our hands.

My sexuality is not, but is limited to:
an outfit change,
reasonable only to *hook-up* in the closet.

First published in 'Beyond Queer Words Anthology'

Spiralled Shell

I have detached myself
from my care for you
in identity, in emotion, in denial
and if that's what it takes to survive
I will float so far away
your heaven will have no choice but to take me.

Until you find: I'm no longer
in the spiralled shell
you made of me,
and too, vacate.

Until, slowly,
the letters of my own name
form a mantra
I can return home to.

First published in 'Australian Poetry Journal, 12.1'

The Nightflower Thief

P.F.

The beautiful Nightflower Thief,

has a compulsion to pick every flower she comes across
and place them on the dashboard
of her car.

At the O'Connell bakery she targets the Jasmine
like she's shoplifting.
Stubbornly pulling it off the bush
and stuffing it in her pocket.

At my house she takes the Abelia,
lifting it to her nose;
a wholesome drug.

On Ninth Avenue
– a neighbourhood exploding in Christmas lights –
we stop for 10 minutes as she fixates on a rose.
Waiting for foot-traffic to lighten
before she darts her hand through the picket fence.

Her name in Sanskrit refers to the full moon
but she's citrus of the sun;
bright, invigorating and
tipping tabasco over absolutely everything,
including her drinks.

A montage of red lipstick;
clothing doused in more colour and patterns
than I thought any material could possibly hold.

Life follows her.

I wonder when she will lift me from her pocket...
Notice, I've always been medicinal –
thistles, weeds;
not the type to distinguish an
arrangement.

Thank you for reading!
If you'd like to leave a review, it would help tremendously.
Reviews can be left online via Amazon and Goodreads.

For all business-related enquiries please email:
slade.enquiries@gmail.com

Milton Keynes UK
Ingram Content Group UK Ltd.
UKHW010938110724
445228UK00004B/273

9 781763 500501